The True You

Pastor Steve Eden

DEDICATION

I would like to dedicate this book to my Lord and Savior Jesus Christ, my wife Stacy, and to all my mentors and spiritual fathers who have sown so much Truth into me over the years. Thank you all so much!

CONTENTS

Chapter 1
The Great Discovery: Truth

Who would have ever thought the truest thing
about you is what God says about you? Sounds
easy enough, right? Only problem is it takes
great humility for us to really believe all God
says about us in His Word (especially when it's
so good)!

In this book, I want to take you on an amazing
journey to seeing yourself how God sees you,
while unveiling your identity in Christ.
Prayerfully, it will be the greatest journey you
have ever taken! Simply DARE TO BELIEVE
that as a born again child of God, your
Heavenly Father actually has fond affection
toward you and longs for you to hear Him say
all kinds of good things about you. Shall we
begin?

**Proverbs 23:7 says, "As a man thinks in his
heart, so is he…"**

Based on this Scripture, how you see yourself is
both crucial and critical as it determines how
you live, act, and interact with others. A very
valid question every human being should be

asking is, "Who is the source of the thoughts and ideas I use to determine what is true about me, about God, about others, and about life?" Is it Oprah? The media? Hollywood? The latest fashions? The government? The internet? Or is it God and His Word? There are so many voices in the world who want to shape who you are by telling you what is 'right', truth, and what you should believe. It reminds me of the Garden of Eden when God asked Adam, "Who told you you were naked?" All He is asking Adam is – "Who is your source of information because I never told you that!"

Knowing your true identity and the source of your true value is very important for Christians because so many simply do not know, or were not taught, what happened to them once Christ's Spirit entered their heart at the new birth. So if you have prayed that old familiar prayer, "Jesus, come into my heart and save me," and/or consider yourself a Christian, this book can be of great use to you. It should give you insight into who you became on the inside the day of your decision for Christ, as well as help you to see yourself how your Heavenly Father sees you.

Let's begin with some wonderful things God has to say about you in His Word:

THE TRUE YOU!

Start each day by agreeing with who God says you are!

I AM:

A child of God (Romans 8:16)

At peace with God (Romans 5:1)

Precious to God (Isaiah 43:3)

Forgiven (Colossians 1:14)

A partaker of God's divine nature (2 Peter 1:3)

More than a conqueror (Romans 8:37)

Loved unconditionally by God (1 John 4:10)

A priest in the Kingdom of God (Revelation 1:6)

Accepted in the beloved (Ephesians 1:6)

Chosen by God (John 15:16)

A joint heir with Jesus (Romans 8:17)

Washed clean by Christ's blood (Revelation 1:5)

Indwelt by God's Spirit (Ezekiel 36:26)

God's Kingdom ambassador (2 Corinthians 5:20)

The Righteousness of God (2 Corinthians 5:21)

One Spirit with Jesus (1 Corinthians 6:17)

Flesh of His flesh & bone of His bone (Ephesians 5:30)

Full of the Glory of God (John 17:22)

The Light of the world (Matthew 5:14)

Born again with an incorruptible seed (1 Peter 1:23)

God's workmanship (Ephesians 2:10)

Redeemed by the blood of the Lamb (1Peter 1:18)

Sealed with the Holy Spirit of Promise (Ephesians 1:13)

Blessed with every spiritual blessing (Ephesians 1:3)

God's new creation (2 Corinthians 5:17)

A minister of the New Covenant (2 Corinthians 3:6)

Complete and qualified in Christ (Colossians 2:10)

A friend of God (John 15:15)

Free from condemnation (Romans 8:1)

Holy, without blame, free from accusation in His sight
(Colossians 1:22)

Having just read all those things that God says you are as a born again Christian, is it any wonder the devil does not like you very much? Is it any wonder he attacks you, your family, your self-worth, your health, your faith, your children, your finances, your church, your relatives, or your spouse? I mean you are clearly a huge threat to the enemy and yet so few Christians would ever see themselves as capable of dealing him or his schemes damaging blows.

I recommend you meditate daily on those verses that detail The True You. Take a good look at them, receive them with all your heart, say them aloud, say them to yourself, say them to the devil or whoever will listen, but APPLY the Truth to yourself! Have faith in who God says you are instead of who everyone else or even your past mistakes say you are.

Cultivate a grateful attitude for the new identity God has given you in Christ. See yourself through His heart for you. At least once each day, remind yourself of who God says you are in His Word. Say for example, "Father, I thank you I am your masterpiece. Thank you I am loved and forgiven. Thank you I am accepted in the beloved."

It seems we struggle as humans with proper value assignment. We typically assign more value to what others say or think about us; or how we personally feel about ourselves than what the God of the universe (who made us) says!! He's the One who is actually the real authority on us, our value, and our potential. Those other people didn't make us, they didn't form us in our mother's womb, they have no idea what our real value and potential is!

3 John 1:3-4 says, "3 For I rejoiced greatly when the brethren came and testified of the truth *that is* in you... 4 <u>I have no greater joy than to hear that my children walk in truth."</u>

Religion and the world want to focus on your actions and getting your behavior modified, but God wants to teach you about walking in truth.

Now I am about to say something really radical, but once you consider it, you will see its merit. Ready? <u>There is truth that exists beyond what you think, feel, or believe about yourself. Just because you do not believe something is true or feel it about yourself doesn't mean it's not really true</u>! Do you think there are many people in the world right now thinking, feeling,

or believing God doesn't love them? Sure there
are! Far too many! Some in church and some
not. Some born again and some not. But what
is the truth? The truth is of course God loves
them, it is who He is! God doesn't just have
love, He is love. 1 John 4:8 verifies this!
Jeremiah 31:3 also proves God's love:

**In Jeremiah 31:3 God says, "I have loved
you with an everlasting love and drawn you
with my loving-kindness."**

Can God lie? No, so then He most certainly
loves you and everyone else on this planet! My
point is, our feelings and opinions can actually
keep us from experiencing the life, joy, and
peace of what is true about us! How sad it
would be if we arrive at Heaven one day
expecting Jesus to say, "Now that you are in
Heaven My child, you are loved and accepted";
but instead we see Jesus' wondrous, love-filled
face and without His saying a word, we know
He has loved and accepted us from day one, but
we simply hadn't believed it.

So let me make this point again – Just because
you choose not to BELIEVE something
awesome God says about you doesn't make it

<u>untrue. Or, just because you choose to BELIEVE something awful about yourself doesn't make it true.</u> We do not determine truth as humans, we only discover truth as humans. The truth was here long before we arrived and the truth will be here long after we are gone. But once we know, participate with, and BELIEVE the truth; we begin experiencing the life, joy, and freedom Jesus promised us!

John 8:31-32 records, "Then Jesus said to those who believed on Him, 'If you abide (live, remain, or stay) in <u>My word</u>, you are My disciples indeed, and you shall <u>know the truth and the truth shall make you free.</u>'"

Jesus didn't say we create or determine the truth, He said the truth is something we come to know. Interestingly, the word "know" in this passage has a participatory connotation to it; it's not just a knowledge 'about' the truth but actually a 'participation' with or 'joining' to the truth. Again, whether we believe the truth about us or not doesn't determine whether it is true; our belief simply allows us to experience the life and freedom of what is true.

It is very important what we think, feel, or believe not become higher authorities (in our mind) than the truth of God's Word! <u>Honestly, the most humble thing you can do is agree with who God says you are</u>.

Once you are born again by the incorruptible seed of the Word of God, the devil cannot make you bad, (after all, Jesus Christ MADE you a righteous, holy, brand new creation), he can only make you think you're bad! Just be aware though, that is precisely his goal. If he can convince you that you are bad through your feelings or beliefs then those feelings and beliefs will negatively and directly impact your actions and habits. After all, as a man thinks in his heart, so is he.

Find some time each day to celebrate the fact that you cannot make yourself more righteous or more loved than Jesus Christ has made you. Consider the reality that: #1) God loves you because He's so good, not because you're so good. #2) He is committed to you because of the purity of His heart, not the purity of yours. #3) Your behavior is not the measure of your acceptance before God, God's unchanging character is!

You may say, "You mean I am still righteous, accepted, and forgiven in Christ even if I mess up?" Yes, even if you mess up. As a new creation in Christ, God made you who you are, not you. Yes, you consented to becoming His child, but He did the making! I find it interesting how people say they believe God loves them unconditionally and has forgiven them of all their sin, but they live as though it's really, "Well, God has forgiven me of all my sin <u>unless</u> I sin again" or "Well, God accepts me unconditionally <u>unless</u> I do something unacceptable."

They think more of their mistakes than they do of His love. They actually believe their actions control HIS character! <u>I always tell people, "Trust me, God is not looking to you to determine who He's gonna be</u>." Isn't it possible, like we do as parents with our children, that God is quite capable of accepting us while not accepting some of our behaviors? Of course.

Now does our behavior matter? No doubt it does. Sin hurts you and will take everything you love if you make it your master. This is because, as humans, we are not designed for sin, but for righteousness. Man and God are affinities, not man and sin. History has proven over and over again that sin is not just bad, it's bad for us! I will speak more on why our behavior matters in chapter 8.

Christians need to see themselves as God sees them because God's perspective is the truthful perspective that not only sets us free but empowers us.

Genesis 6:8 says "Noah found <u>GRACE</u> in the <u>EYES</u> of the Lord."

It is so amazing the supernatural empowerment (that is what grace is) we find in any given situation when we start seeing ourselves as God does. I strongly recommend we see ourselves through His eyes; not the eyes of our flesh, our feelings, or the views and opinions of others.

<u>As children of God and new creations in Christ, we do not get to determine who and what we are, we only get to discover who and what we are by the Holy Spirit!</u> That, my friends, makes the Christian life an exciting journey!

Pastor Steve Eden

Chapter 2
Salvation with a Side of Security Please...

Through the years of my various religious experiences, I would hear the good news of God's offer of salvation. Unfortunately, it seemed the good news quickly ended and the bad news began once I decided to get saved. If you've ever felt like I did -- that the good news was just for lost man, this chapter is for you.

Spirit, Soul, and Body

Just like God is a triune being, one God comprised of three parts; I believe man is a triune being, one man comprised of three parts.

This is a revelation that, as you get it, will absolutely open the Scriptures to you. It will also give you some much needed security in your relationship with God; providing you a salvation to work FROM instead of one to work for. After all, the Apostle Paul in Philippians 2:12 said work OUT your salvation; not work for it. Lastly and prayerfully, by understanding spirit-soul-body, you will be able to grasp why even though God says you are holy, you still act unholy on occasion.

God's Dwelling Place

Just like the Old Testament "tabernacle" (dwelling place) had three parts – Holy of Holies, Most Holy Place, and Outer Court; we as humans have three parts: Spirit, Soul, and Body. The tabernacle was one of the places in the Old Testament where God's Spirit took up temporary housing until Jesus finished rebuilding the new temple (you); as He mentioned He would do in John 2:21.

There are 50 chapters in the Old Testament devoted to Moses building God a tabernacle that contains three parts-- I think that is because God the Father wanted to give you some insight (through type & shadow) into the three part tabernacle Christ was going to build in the New Testament. You are God's temple now, as seen in 1 Corinthians 3:16 and 1 Corinthians 6:19.

1 Thessalonians 5:23 says "May God himself, the God of peace, sanctify you through and through. May your whole <u>spirit, soul, and body</u> be kept blameless at the coming of our Lord Jesus Christ."

This passage confirms we are 3-part beings. As a born again Christian, your spirit man is righteous, sanctified, one with Christ, and redeemed. That's the real you. Your soul is comprised of your mind, your will (your choice mechanism), and your emotions. Your body is your earth suit, shell, or outer container.

In Ezekiel 36:26-27 God says, "I will give you a new heart and put a new spirit in you; I will remove from you your heart of stone and give you a heart of flesh. 27 <u>And I will put my Spirit in you</u> and move you to follow my decrees and be careful to keep my laws."

This passage is a fore-telling of what was to come in the New Covenant. <u>It is truly amazing that God puts His very Spirit INSIDE us at the new birth.</u> Once you are made new as God's child, just as you have natural characteristics of your natural father, so also, you receive the spiritual characteristics of your spiritual Father. His very DNA of love, holiness, peace, and righteousness have been placed inside you. You are born of His Spirit (John 3:6)!

2 Corinthians 5:17 says, "Behold if any man is in Christ, he is a new creation, old things have passed away; behold all things have become new."

God makes us 'new creations' in our spirit, not our soul or body. Notice when someone gets 'saved' or accepts Christ into their heart, they don't lose their free will or emotions; nor does their weight, height, or eye color change; it's their inner man that is changed. If you weighed 200 pounds with a bald head when you received Christ, then you weighed 200 pounds with a bald head afterward!

Adam and Eve didn't die physically after they ate the forbidden fruit – Adam lived to be 930 years old. They didn't die soulically either because they could still make choices and show emotions afterward. They died spiritually. They still had a spirit but it was no longer alight or alive with God's life. So this is why Christ coming to give us life (John 10:10) is huge because our dead spirits could be, dare we say it, "born again"!

How about a little security?

1 Corinthians 6:17 says as believers we are "one spirit with Christ." Because of this union, our new spirit man has never sinned nor will ever sin because it's one with the very Spirit of Jesus. 1 John 3:9 now makes sense, "No one

who is born of God practices sin, because His seed abides in him; and <u>he cannot sin, because he is born of God</u>." Wow, a born again believer cannot sin by our new spirit within! Keep in mind though, we can create many a calamity and misdeed when we operate out of an un-renewed mind, the flesh, or our emotions.

Hebrews 12:23 says, "the SPIRITS of just men made perfect..."

Notice it's your spirit that has been made perfect. One-third of your salvation is complete! Your spirit is saved, your soul is being saved (see James 1:21, 1 Peter 1:9, & Hebrews 10:39), and your body will be saved at the second coming of the Lord. Unfortunately many doctrines today still teach man as only two parts: soul and body. Hence, there is so much performance-based Christianity today because there's no finished part of our salvation. Everybody's living like they're earning something instead of living like they've received something.

<u>Think of your union with Christ in your spirit like making tea.</u> If you have a glass of water (you), and then you put a tea bag in it (Christ's Spirit), the resulting "new creation" is called, "tea". Why? Because a union has happened

between the water and the tea. You can't tell where the tea begins and the water ends. They are one. So it is with you and Christ! When His righteousness hits our unrighteousness, it's tea baby! "We be tea" not that old stale, dirty water we used to be!

When you understand what happened in your spirit at the new birth, you have a secure identity from which to work from and share Christ with others. And let's face it, plants grow better and bear more fruit when they stay securely planted instead of being uprooted and re-planted every other day.

2 Corinthians 5:18-19 says, "Now all things *are* of God, <u>who has reconciled us to Himself through Jesus Christ, and has given us the ministry of reconciliation,</u> 19 that is, that God was in Christ reconciling the world to Himself, not imputing their trespasses to them, and has committed to us the word of reconciliation."

Do you think God would give us the ministry of reconciliation, if we were not already reconciled? If I am not assured of my own reconciliation with God, how can I share it confidently with others? If I think my mistakes make God distance Himself from me because

He is unhappy with me, why would I tell others they can be clean and close to God without reservation? Folks are confused when our message does not match our own beliefs.

<u>We are designed to REFLECT our reconciliation and intimacy with God, not create it.</u> Feeling reconciled is not the same as knowing we are reconciled. Feelings can change; God and His Word do not. When we are assured of our reconciliation, we will turn and confidently offer it to others. God gave Christ into the world because He knew man would never offer peace to other men until he was at peace with himself, but God also knew man couldn't be at peace with himself until he really believed he was at peace with God. Enter Christ's gift of peace described in Romans 5:1 which says, "Therefore, having been justified by faith, <u>we have peace with god through our Lord Jesus Christ</u>."

We've spent far too long trying to become something we already are. Too long trying to get something (reconciliation) that we already have. <u>Until you know who's keeping you, you'll look to everyone else to keep you: Keep you happy, keep you reconciled, keep you valuable, keep you going.</u>

Philemon 1:6 says, "I pray that the communication of your faith may become effective through the knowledge of EVERY good thing which is in you in Christ..."

Maybe your momma didn't tell you, maybe your pastor didn't tell you, maybe your spouse didn't tell you but I'm gonna tell you: God has put a whole lot of good inside of you in Christ! What's in your spirit is molecule for molecule the DNA of God! You'll never face anything outside of you greater than Who is inside of you!

It is amazing how our faith becomes effective and communicable when we actually acknowledge all the good Christ has brought to our spirit man rather than seeing only the bad we do, or moping around wondering if we've done enough today to stay saved! Perhaps the key to a transformed outer life is simply the acknowledgement that we actually have a transformed inner life!

Your spirit man being made righteous is now the absolute, the constant, that you and Christ can build together from. An 80 year old minister in Florida, after getting a revelation of the new birth for the very first time said, "For sixty years I've served God out of what I could do for Him, but today I begin serving Him out of what He did for me." He found rest! He found security! He realized He had a new righteous identity! And did it make him want to sin more? Absolutely not – just the opposite. His heart was filled with gratitude, love, humility, and praise.

<u>Now for some sanity and clarity on why some scriptures say I am saved and holy, and others say I'm being saved and made holy:</u>

Hebrews 10:14 says, "For by one sacrifice Christ <u>has made</u> perfect forever those who <u>are being made</u> holy."

This passage would be highly confusing if you don't understand spirit, soul, and body, because it is clear part of me has been 'perfected forever' (past tense), and yet part of me is being 'made holy' (present tense). My spirit is what was made perfect in Christ; my soul (mind, will, emotions) is what is being made holy.

1 Peter 1:8-9 says, "Though now you do not see *Him*, yet believing, you rejoice with joy inexpressible and full of glory, 9 receiving the end result of your faith—the salvation of *your* souls."

As you can see, the end result of our faith (participating with all that God's grace has provided), is the salvation not of our spirit, but our soul. Like leaven (see Matthew 13:33), Christ begins in our spirit at the new birth, but then desires to save and sanctify our mind, thoughts, choices, and emotions over time. Jesus' parable in Matthew 13:33 is a perfect illustration of how the Spirit of God works within us as a triune being, moving from one part until all three parts of us are leavened.

James 1:21 says, "Therefore lay aside all filthiness and overflow of wickedness, and receive with meekness the implanted word, which is able to save your souls."

Notice our meekness and humility towards God's implanted Word (Christ) is able to save our soul (doesn't say our spirit). That's because Christ has been implanted in our spirit and from there leavens our soul and body; transforming us and conforming us in every way to Himself. What a wonderful partnership! His power and character at work and manifesting through our simple willingness, agreement, and humility!

It is also worth noting the Holy Spirit in the Bible has a male connotation and our soul has a female connotation. We see the Holy Spirit portrayed as a "He" in Luke 4:18 and John 14:16 while our soul is termed a "her" in Psalm 34:2 (KJV). <u>So we conclude that the Spirit of God sows, the soul of man receives, that the body may birth (give form to, and evidence of, the Life conceived within).</u>

Romans 12:1-2 says, "1 I beseech you therefore, brethren, by the mercies of God, that you present your <u>bodies</u> a living sacrifice, holy, acceptable to God, *which is* your reasonable service. 2 And do not be conformed to this world, but be transformed by the renewing of your <u>mind</u>, that you may prove what *is* that good and acceptable and perfect will of God."

Notice in this prominent New Testament passage, Paul makes no mention of transforming your spirit man because it's your soul and body that are still in the process of being sanctified. While the power of the Christian life does not come from the mind, it does come through the mind. You can't just let your thoughts go unchecked and un-renewed or this world and the enemy will clean your clock.

The renewing of your mind is critical because while it is easy to become a born again Christian, it can be beyond difficult to change

your thinking! <u>That's why there are so many
Scriptures that deal with the mind: Renew your
mind, be of the same mind, you have the mind
of Christ, be renewed in the spirit of your mind,
set your mind, God gives soundness of mind,
think on these things, let this mind be in you,
and my personal favorite – Romans 8:6, the
mind set on the spirit is life and peace!</u>

Your new birth was quick, bringing your dead
spirit to life was quick, but <u>changing</u> some of
your wrong thinking and perspectives is gonna
take a while! Guiding you into the reality of
truth is gonna take a while. But hear this: It is a
process that Christ within you, via the Person of
the Holy Spirit is committed to completing.

If your spirit has all these amazing things God
says it has, but your mind doesn't get renewed
and aligned to it, then you are robbed not from
the reality of what is in your spirit but from
experiencing the benefits and empowerment of
what is in your spirit. <u>Thus, an un-renewed
mind is how God can make you righteous as
His child, but yet you still do unrighteous
things from time to time.</u> Your mind set on the
spirit will produce good spiritual fruit while
your mind set on the flesh will produce the
deeds of the flesh. As I will touch on later, it is

simply 2 on 1 in favor of the flesh or the Spirit based upon where our mind is aligned.

What is amazing according to Romans 12:2 is when you do align your mind with who you are by the spirit, that's when you and your body start proving how good, acceptable, and perfect God's will is! Why is God's will good, acceptable, and perfect for you? Because you are made by God and FOR God (Colossians 1:16). Your participation with your Heavenly Father will always have a sense of homecoming on it, never estrangement. Quite simply, He made you for Himself, His Word, and His will.

Pastor Steve Eden

Chapter 3
What If I Stumble, What If I fall?

How you respond to failure, adversity, and disappointment in your walk with Christ is probably one of the most neglected but needed topics in all of Christianity. As Christians, while we have the privilege of being made holy and right with God, we often feel the responsibility of being those who've been made holy and right with God. So when missteps occur, many times we are the first one to lay the wood to ourselves; putting the accuser of the brethren out of a job!

Additionally, let me say this – yes, even though we are children of God, born of God's very Spirit, we are quite capable of committing some real blunders along life's journey. Our misbehaviors, especially until we really mature in Christ, can be painful, disappointing, and even tragic at times, so we have to be able to 'get up off the mat' and respond properly.

Proverbs 24:16 says, "The godly may trip seven times, but they get up again."

It never ceases to amaze me how many

Christians simply give up after a failure. How is that an alternative? Just go on living estranged from God in your own mind, doing it all on your own? No thanks. We have no hope of getting back to walking in righteousness again apart from walking with the Lord. The enemy is just trying to get you to judge yourself unworthy of the only One who can help you get back on track and lead you into a life of fullness and freedom.

Some people if they don't give up take on the "Bunkhouse mentality." We see this in Luke 15 when the prodigal son, after a period of loose living, sells His Father's goodness and love so far short that he asks to be his Father's servant and no longer his son! He assigns so much value to his sins that he assumes his own Father has disowned him and wants nothing to do with him.

I'm sure the prodigal was thinking as so many Christians do today, "Father I know we can never be close again because I'm so bad, so please just let me serve you at arms length from now on." You'll notice though, the Father didn't even let the boy get his request out before He ran to him, tackled him, and restored his son-ship!

In the nineties, the Christian band DC Talk put out a song with the lyrics:

"What if I stumble, what if I fall?

What if I lose my step and make fools of us all?

Will the love continue when the walk becomes a crawl?

What if I stumble, what if I fall?"

A very valid question for sure. The song was questioning whether fans would still love the band members if they had a moral failure, but the thought and question certainly applies to God too. How many people, due to their struggles in life have ever wondered where God is concerned, "Will the love continue?"

If I've learned anything through all my failures over the years, it is that God is faithful and committed to see me, my sanctification, and my maturity in Christ through to completion.

Philippians 1:6 says, "Being confident of this very thing, that He who has begun a good work in you, He will complete *it* until the day of Jesus Christ…"

Notice He <u>WILL</u> complete it! Some versions say He is 'faithful' to complete it. That means you can now relax, you're not going to be God's first failure. The Lord told me once, "Steve, I never start anything I haven't already finished." Wow, He had us completed in Christ from before the foundations of the world! God has always been able to see our end from the beginning.

Dealing with temptation, sin, missteps, disappointment and the like:

First of all, on the front end of any temptation keep in mind: Your new creation spirit not only cannot sin (1 John 3:9), but it doesn't even like sin! When temptation comes, just know your spirit man wants nothing to do with it. Recognize it and say – "That is not who I am. It will not satisfy me. I am too great a creation to be satisfied by sin. I am predestined to be conformed to Christ; therefore, what looks good on Him looks good on me. I am righteous and I am made for righteousness."

As for overcoming feelings of disappointment because you did some incredible piece of stupid, it always helped me to ask myself, "What good is it going to do you or anyone else to stay here in the hole of no impact beating yourself up? What good is wallowing? Why not get up, rise again, and start partnering with God again!" That mindset will always help far more than a day of self-pity followed by a night of self-loathing.

If and when you do commit a sin (miss the mark), immediately renew your mind to agree with God about your standing with Him in the midst of your difficulty and 'guilty' feelings. Turn from unbelief and instead agree with who God still says you are. Dare to believe your poor choice did not change your spirit man's relationship and union with Christ inside. Rise up with the understanding, an apple tree is STILL an apple tree even if there are no apples on it right now.

When you stumble, remember you still have the power of choice. Freedom to choose allows a person to reveal who their heart really loves! Stand up and say, "I will not be moved off my true identity again! I choose to renew my mind to who I am in Christ and who I really love!" Obviously to do a "big piece of stupid" means our mind wasn't renewed to our identity in Christ anyway; because it is very difficult to commit a sin while humbly thinking in your heart how amazingly righteous you are.

After a poor choice, the enemy will say you are not qualified to fellowship with God, be used of God, or to be His child anymore. He will tell you that you have changed back to being an old sinner. <u>But understand one wrong behavior cannot disqualify you or change your identity any more than one right behavior qualifies you or saves you</u>! Committing a sin doesn't make you a sinner any more than committing a righteous deed makes you righteous. We are either qualified by Christ's life, spirit, and blood or we are not qualified!

The enemy will also try to tell you that you must do something righteous to become righteous again. <u>Be very careful when you set out to become something though, because you just told yourself you're not something.</u> Look at Adam and Eve. They were 'like God' having been made in God's image and yet the devil tempted them by saying, "If you eat of this tree, you'll be 'like God'," so he tempted them to become something they already were!

This happens in churches every Sunday. Christians ask God to love them, bless them, or even make them holy again when the whole time they already were all those things in Christ. What happened? Unbelief happened.

Romans 14:23 says, "Anything not from faith is sin."

Adam and Eve did not believe in that moment they were "like" God or they would have laughed at the devil's offer. If there's a HUGE sin the American church struggles with, it's not some act we commit here or there, it's all the unbelief about our identity in Christ and who God says we are that leads to those acts. <u>We simply must know in our heart that the union that has happened with Christ in our spirit man is the greater reality and more true than what our outer man does at times.</u>

1 Peter 1:23 says, "Having been born again, not of a corruptible seed but incorruptible, by the Word of God that lives and abides forever."

Contrary to what so many believe -- your outer behavior cannot undo your inner identity. You cannot corrupt the seed of righteousness within you. You've been born again by an incorruptible (imperishable) Seed! Look up the word incorruptible in your dictionary and you may just break into your own personal revival!! Remember with great joy it is what's true about you!

You've been born again not of a performance or of a self-made righteousness, but of the incorruptible seed of Christ! My security as a believer then is not in myself; it's in what God has done in me, and I can bank on that!

Chapter 4
Three Major Strongholds, Six Major Truths

In this chapter, let's look at three major "strongholds" (beliefs and ideas that determine behavior) which really hinder God's people; and six major truths that protect us from deception.

Three Major Strongholds:

Stronghold #1 - Separation Theology. This belief is that God is way off in heaven somewhere, lofty and aloof, and we are down here trying to do our very best for Him. In other words, there is no understanding of Colossians 1:27.

Colossians 1:27 says, "God has chosen me to make known the mystery, which is <u>Christ IN YOU</u> the hope of glory."

<u>While it is true God is everywhere and certainly present in Heaven and beyond, it is important to recognize the very presence of Christ within us.</u>

It is laughable that any Christian would think we could be like God apart from Him. So Christ came, went to the cross and eradicated our sin. In that bold and loving act, Jesus cleansed God's original temple (us) so His Spirit could take up residence within whosoever would receive Him. The idea we are separate from Christ leads us into a lot of self-striving and burnout. We live too much of our Christian lives in our own efforts to 'get close' to the Lord instead of living and loving from Him as our ever present, internal Supply.

If you are not saved, you simply need to invite Christ to come in. Let Him know that His precious Spirit is welcome to be Lord of your heart. We are <u>not</u> saved by the cross and remission of our sin; we are saved when God's Spirit moves inside and "life's" our dead spirit. When that happens, you are born again. Imagine, saved by simple receptivity not religious activity! Now you're ready to reveal a life that's clean and close to God!

Because Christ lives in you, you can now love from the love HE supplies. You can now live holy from the holiness HE supplies. No fear of ever running out of anything you need. When you get Him, you get all you need for life and Godliness (righteousness, holiness, love, mercy, etc...). <u>You should never try to get by behavior what God has given you freely in Christ!!</u>

Ephesians 2:8-9 says, "8 For by grace you have been saved through faith, and that not of yourselves; *it is* the gift of God, 9 not of works, lest anyone should boast."

Romans 4:3-5 adds, "3 For what does the Scripture say? "Abraham believed God, and it was accounted to him for righteousness." 4 Now to him who works, the wages are not counted as grace but as debt. 5 But to him who does not work but believes on Him who justifies the ungodly, his faith is accounted for righteousness."

You have been given salvation as a gift in the person of Jesus Christ. You no longer have to believe the lie that you are separate from Him because Jesus said, "Lo, I am with you always, even until the end of the age."

Romans 8:10 says, "10 And if Christ *is* in you, the body *is* dead because of sin, but the Spirit *is* life because of righteousness."

Galatians 2:20 says, "I have been crucified with Christ; it is no longer I who live, but Christ lives in me…"

Stronghold #2 - Performance-based Acceptance. This belief says if you do good, God will love you; but if you don't do good, He won't love you. God's love is never performance based. He loves you because of who He is; not because of what you do! As I mentioned before, God loves you because He is love; it has nothing to do with you or your behavior.

God is just looking for someone to believe in His character. I say character because God does not put His character or behavior in your hands. He's not looking to you to determine whether He loves you or not-- that is just arrogance for you to think you have the power to control God's character. Again, our behavior matters in terms of sin, as it hurts us and hurts those we love, but it does not determine whether God loves us or accepts us. He may not accept or like all of our behavior, but even through failure, we remain an accepted, loved, new creation in Christ.

<u>We cannot get caught thinking more highly of our mistakes than we do of God's faithfulness.</u> How do you have intimacy with someone you believe will turn on you or abort you when you fail? It is interesting that the same people who

will preach hell hot that God hates abortion will turn around and tell God's children He would abort them if they fail or become "inconvenient" to Him. If God loved us enough to die for us as His enemies (Romans 5:8), how much more will He love us through our mistakes as His children!

If you are trying to get God to love you, you are too late. He already loves you with a love that will never fail. He loved you before you were born. He even loved you before you started trying to get Him to love you! Your behavior cannot create love inside a God who already IS love. You are NOT on a date with God, trying by your actions to create love inside of someone for you that you hope will last. You are in covenant with a covenant-keeping God. You cannot manipulate/obligate God into loving you more than He already does.

Growing up, I believed the lie that Christianity was all about me and my performance. In my mind, I was self-righteous when my behavior was good, unrighteous when it was bad. I was definitely at the center of my Christianity-- not Christ. I felt accepted or unaccepted by God based upon my own knowledge of good and evil; which led to a lot of grief and frustration.

Stronghold #3 – Performance-based Identity.
This belief is that our identity is directly tied to
our conduct. It is the idea that what I do
determines who I am. If I do bad, then I am
bad. If I do good, then I am good. If I tell a lie,
then I'm a liar. Simply put, this deception thinks
we, by our behavior, determine our identity and
value to God instead of God and His Word. It
says I have to DO something to become
something, and that my behavior is a higher law
and authority than God's truth.

What you do does NOT determine who you are.
The reverse is true: who you are determines
what you do. Who you are in your spirit, your
inner man where Christ and His righteousness
now reside, that is the true you. When we
accept this Truth, become one with it, renew
our minds to it, then we manifest it.

Our problem is we like to "yeah but" the truth
with our behavior rather than "yeah but" our
behavior with the truth! Perhaps you're familiar
with this inner dialogue: "Yeah I know 2
Corinthians 5:21 says I am righteous, but what I
did yesterday sure wasn't righteous." Let's turn
that around: "Yeah I know what I did yesterday
wasn't righteous, but 2 Corinthians 5:21 says I
am righteous!" With that second statement

comes the grace and empowerment we need going forward.

<u>The idea that your actions determine your identity is so crippling to your intimacy with God</u>. The enemy likes to snapshot a wrong behavior, then try to identify you as that wrong behavior. We must resist the devil and know God and the spirit identity He gave us inwardly doesn't fluctuate with our outer missteps.

Look at it this way… A bird does not become a bird when it starts to fly. A bird is a bird at its birth. In the same way, God doesn't wait to call you a righteous, holy, new creation-Christian once you start acting like one. He calls you that at your new birth! He gives you a new heart and a new nature that aligns with your new identity, then says, "With these I will now show you how to fly!"

I may not always act as if I am righteous or always believe it, but it is Truth. My true nature is based on Christ in my spirit. I cannot act or behave my way to righteousness. Maybe you've heard, "You have to go to church to be righteous." "You have to tithe to be righteous." Behavior becomes the focus; duty becomes the motive, burnout and an identity crisis become the fruit.

As I mentioned before, once you set out to become something, you just told yourself you're not something. And if you are setting out to become something (holy) that God's Word already says you are, you are in unbelief—yes, even if you are doing Christian things to become it. I am fine with you doing good works: Praying, abstaining from big pieces of stupid, going to church; but do them because you are holy not to become holy.

The Spirit of God living in you is God's total answer to your total need. The deceiver will say you are what you do. He will say your identity is performance based, not Christ based; because he knows that if you ever discover how righteous you are in Christ, your performance will begin to radically improve.

Six Major Truths:

Truth #1 - *There is Truth that exists beyond what you think, feel, or believe about yourself.*

For example, God loves you whether you believe He does or not. <u>Faith doesn't make God love you, faith allows you to experience the life and peace of God's love towards you.</u> No one wants to live out a lie (from a false reality); yet too many believers live, walk, and relate to God by what they feel or think is true about their identity rather than God's opinion. Your perspective is your reality, so make sure it's God's perspective.

Truth #2 - *The truest thing about you is what God says about you.*

Not what anyone else says about you -- not even what you say about you or your behavior says about you. The truth was here long before any of us arrived and will be here long after we are gone. As humans, we do not determine what is true about us, we only discover what is true about us. Once we know and participate with it, it sets us free!

Truth #3 - *The most humble thing you can do is agree with who God says you are.*

When we live by our own opinions, feelings, or thoughts about ourselves that disagree with God, that is ultimately pride. It insinuates we know more about our worth and potential than our Manufacturer does. It reveals we are looking to ourselves for our identity and value instead of Him. <u>Pride in its purest form is self-centeredness instead of Christ-centeredness.</u>

Truth #4 - *God not only will not lie, He cannot lie (Titus 1:2).*

If God said tomorrow, "The sky is brown" it would turn brown! Simply because what He says is true. God has a lot of good things to say about you, so dare to believe what He says no matter how good it is. If He says you've been made righteous through Christ (2 Corinthians 5:21), then it must be true, so agree with Him! If He says you are accepted in the beloved (Ephesians 1:6), it must be true so believe Him! The highest and most infallible authority in the universe is God's Word.

Truth #5 - *Knowing the Truth will set you free, therefore believing a lie will set you in bondage.*

Think about it: If a person believes the lie they are unloveable, no good, and will never amount to anything, they are not going to find or experience much freedom. It's in their divine design to believe they are lovely, good, and valuable. You might think your bondage is from a sinful behavior, but the lie that produced that behavior is the problem. Starting with believing the chief lie that a sinful behavior could satisfy you. You are too great a creation to be satisfied by anything but the Spirit of

God. Colossians 1:16 says every human being is made by God AND for God. He formed you so He could dwell IN you and express His Life THROUGH you. Anytime we humans think we can run on something outside of Christ and His Truth, it is like a car trying to run on orange juice instead of gasoline. <u>By creative design, for optimum performance, gas goes in the car, oil goes in the lamp, and Christ goes in the human being.</u>

Truth #6 - *The words and thoughts we believe about ourselves are like seeds that grow in our heart.*

I will never forget an 8 year old girl who overheard her mother say to a friend on the phone, "I wish she'd never been born". That little girl took those words and believed them, she let them grow in <u>the soil of her heart</u> (Jesus revealed words are like seeds and our hearts like soil in Matthew 13:19). For the next five years she lived angrily and rebelliously as one who believed she had no value, purpose, or significance in this world. But at age 13, a Christian counsellor began meeting with the troubled and trouble-making girl and diagnosed the root of bitterness causing all the fruit of misbehavior. He explained to her how God is the One who determines her real value and worth in this world, and that while she came through her mother, she really came FROM God! He shared with her words of truth and the significance she had in Christ. She took those words and believed them. They entered her heart and shattered the darkness and deception she had formerly believed. From that day forward she began to live freely and lovingly as one who saw herself and others as precious in the eyes of God.

Chapter 5
The War Over Identification: Flesh or Spirit

Many times we struggle with knowing ourselves after the flesh and our performance instead of by the Spirit. Doesn't it make sense that if God is Spirit, and He is (John 4:24), He would see and know us by the spirit, and desire we see and know ourselves the same way?

We must come out of the mindset that my performance defines me, my clothes define me, my skin color defines me, my social class defines me. No, who God says I am defines me!

2 Corinthians 5:16 says, "From now on, we know no man after the flesh..."

Even Paul instructs us not to know our fellow believers by the flesh but by the spirit, so I can assure you he desires us to know ourselves by the spirit as well.

The devil wants you to recognize yourself by how you perform in the flesh, yet the flesh isn't the end all revelation of truth. Jesus called the Holy Spirit the "Spirit of Truth" in John chapters 14, 15, and 16. I believe this keynotes both the Spirit's congruence with and revelation of the truth. 1 John 5:6 goes so far as to say, "The Spirit is the truth." It is not a stretch at all then to say the Spirit holds the real reality about us-- not the flesh or it's behaviors.

When you believe on Christ for the remission of sin, recognizing your need of reconciliation to God, He gives you the gift of Himself via His Spirit.

1 Corinthians 6:19 says, "Do you not know that your body is a temple of the Holy Spirit within you, whom you have from God?"

1 Thessalonians 4:8 says, "God has given us His Holy Spirit."

You were <u>not</u> saved by the Cross – you were saved when you received the gift of God's Spirit internally. That is when you were born again and became His child. As a result, you now have a direct line of communication, truth, and lineage to God your Father – the Holy Spirit (the Spirit of Truth).

<u>You will not succeed in communing with God and participating with His Truth about you if you're constantly seeing yourself in the flesh.</u> God relates to us through the Spirit He placed within us. The Father is Spirit and He begot us

as children of His Spirit. That's where we need to abide, in order to connect and relate to God and know ourselves properly.

John 4:24 says, "God is Spirit and those who worship Him must worship Him in Spirit and in truth."

The deception is we think that we are just carnal/physical beings instead of children of God by His Spirit; we too often believe the lie that what happens in the physical realm of behavior is more real or true than what God did in our spirit. It is important we see we are <u>not</u> earthly beings having temporary spiritual experiences, but we are spiritual beings having temporary earthly experiences.

You are born again by God's Spirit; therefore, you are designed to walk by God's Spirit.

Galatians 5:25 says, "Since we've been made alive by the Spirit, let us walk by the Spirit."

Romans 8:14 says, "For those who are led by the Spirit of God, these are the children of God."

See yourself as a spirit-led being, and walk as a spirit-led being. You are designed to receive truth from God's Word and Spirit. They together will correct you, guide you, and caution you when the enemy is trying to deceive you or lie to you.

In John 16:13 Jesus says, "But He, when the Spirit of truth comes, He will guide you into all truth."

Knowing ourselves by and through the Spirit is God's desire, yet the schemes of the devil bank upon us viewing ourselves, and each other, after the flesh. You are not the sum total of your performance though. You are God's new creation. Let the Holy Spirit guide you into the truth about who you really are. <u>Humbly agreeing with God will do far more to subdue your fleshly enticements than all your self-effort.</u>

Evil and unrighteous deeds do not appeal to your Spirit man. They do <u>not</u> fit the new creation you. There's no satisfaction, no fulfillment in the true you to fulfill a temptation to the flesh. The Spirit man evaluates temptation and finds it empty. The lure of money, drugs, sexual perversion, or pornography holds no lure or sway over your Spirit man. Addictions will never satisfy a child of God. You are too great a creation to be satisfied by anything but God. God designed you that way when He made you in His 'likeness' (Genesis 5:1). You cannot change this about yourself because you didn't make yourself, so you may as well accept it.

In summary, know yourself like the One who created you and knows you best. You are who you are, not because of what the flesh has done, but because of what Christ has done.

Pastor Steve Eden

Chapter 6
The Divine Interpreter – The Holy Spirit

In John 14:26 Jesus said, "But the Helper, the Holy Spirit, whom the Father will send in my name, He will teach you all things and will remind you of everything I have said to you."

Ever struggle understanding what someone else is saying? Perhaps they were speaking a foreign language, or speaking too fast, or had a deep accent. Well in much the same way, we can struggle at times to understand what God is saying to us. <u>After all, God speaks spirit. No, He doesn't speak English, Hebrew, or even Greek.</u> God speaks spirit while we speak human, and fallen human at that. So unless we have a spirit like unto God that can discern, interpret, and translate, we are going to find it very difficult to comprehend what He is saying.

You can find many instances in the Gospels where Jesus would share a spiritual truth and His disciples would have no idea what He meant. They, not yet having been born again, did not have the Divine Interpreter (the Holy Spirit) in them to discern and translate. Because of that, Jesus stressed the importance of the Holy Spirit coming to them to, "teach you all things" and "guide you into all truth."

<u>The Christian life is undeniably identification with and comprehension of the things of the Spirit</u>. Jesus was conceived in Mary's womb by the Spirit. Jesus was empowered for ministry by the Spirit. He cast out devils by the Spirit. The Church was birthed in Acts by the Spirit. We are born again by the Spirit. We are changed from glory to glory by the Spirit. We are endued with power from on high by the Spirit. We bear fruit by the Spirit. We worship in spirit. God Himself is Spirit.

Yet all the realities of the Spirit are foolishness to the natural man. The natural man cannot receive or comprehend the things of God's spirit. Even the love of Christ surpasses human knowledge (Ephesians 3:19). In other words, the love of Christ is so unconditional, so steadfast, so faithful, so relentless, and literally so 'not of this world' – it cannot be grasped by our carnal minds.

1 Corinthians 1:18 says, "For the message of the cross is foolishness to those who are perishing, but to us who are being saved it is the power of God."

Self-giving love is the hallmark of the cross, and makes no sense to natural man. The world thinks power is when you take a life, but Jesus revealed real power is when you give your life. That same self-giving love has been placed inside us by the Holy Spirit (Romans 5:5).

Rational human thinking cannot fathom loving people who don't love you or giving your life for your enemies. But think about it, if we are only capable of loving those who give us love to love them with, we are no different than heathen. In Matthew 5:43-48, Jesus accentuates this point in hopes that we will recognize God has higher aims for us than reliance upon the behavior of others to stimulate how we act. He wants us to recognize we have a Source in the Spirit that people of the world just do not have and do not understand.

Christ's constant love for us releases us into the super-natural ability to love others without condition (as He does). A love based on who we are not who others are. A love based on the purity of our heart not theirs. This principle is revealed in John 13:34 when Jesus said, "Love one another just as I love you." Notice He didn't say, "Love people just AS they love you."

Because society is accustomed to, "Whatever you do to me, I will do to you," the things of God may sound just a bit crazy to the people of this world or to a carnal, un-renewed mind. Thank God for the Holy Spirit who guides us into all truth and gives us the super natural understanding we need! Do not let people say you are just 'in the dark' when it comes to the things of God and His Spirit.

1 Corinthians 2:9-10 says, "9 Eye has not seen, nor ear heard, Nor have entered into the heart of man the things which God has prepared for those who love Him. 10 But God has revealed *them* to us through His Spirit. For the Spirit searches all things, yes, the deep things of God."

Most people quote verse 9 apparently without ever seeing verse 10. They make the point that what God has for us is just too amazing for us to ever grasp. While that is true in regard to our carnal mind; our spirit sees, receives, and understands a lot of great revelation -- including who we are in Christ. According to verse 10, God HAS revealed the incredible mysteries of verse 9 to us through His Spirit!

1 Corinthians 2:11 says, "For what man knows the things of a man except the spirit of the man which is in him? Even so no one knows the things of God except the Spirit of God."

Truly your new creation identity is a "thing of God", so the only way you can understand it is by the Spirit of God. Not by your feelings, emotions, or natural rationale. Since when have any of those been the highest authority for discerning truth? <u>Your emotions can't even tell if a movie is real, don't bank on them</u>! You are sitting there in a theatre experiencing fear because you're watching a scary movie and yet truthfully there's nothing real about it – just actors on a screen.

1 Corinthians 2:12 adds, "Now we have received, not the spirit of the world, but the Spirit who is from God, that we might know the things that have been freely given to us by God."

Again, these passages are so amazing! We have been given God's Spirit! We are His very children! Then He mentions that we have received God's Spirit so we 'might know all the things that have been freely given to us'. Notice it's not so we can work for or earn everything.

That has always confused me – I receive Jesus
Christ inside of me but His love, acceptance,
forgiveness, healing, and even my new identity
are not included? God is not holding your
identity or anything else hostage from you.
When you got Jesus, you got it all!

**1 Corinthians 2:13-14 concludes, "13 These
things we also speak, not in words which
man's wisdom teaches but which the Holy
Spirit teaches, comparing spiritual things
with spiritual. 14 <u>But the natural man does
not receive the things of the Spirit of God,
for they are foolishness to him</u>; nor can he
know *them,* because they are spiritually
discerned."**

And there's my point in verse 14. When it
comes to the things of God: Your salvation,
your new creation identity, your complete and
total forgiveness in Christ for example; they're
just not going to make sense to your carnal
mind. They must be discerned and understood
with the help of the Helper (the Holy Spirit).
Again, our feelings and emotions, as well as the
opinions and views of our natural man just will
not be able to see the truth, know the truth,
comprehend the truth, or participate with the
truth.

Always rely on the internal presence of the Holy Spirit, the Spirit of Truth. He lives and loves to be your Teacher and help you not fall prey to any lie-based thinking. Whether that lie is about you and your identity, about God, about His Word, about others, or about life in general on this planet.

Pastor Steve Eden

Chapter 7
Tool Time!

In this chapter, I want to help you walk in the reality of who God says you are by providing you some practical tools that have really proven beneficial to me in my walk with Christ.

Tool #1: Carve out time to listen to God's voice and feed on His Word.

Psalm 85:8 says, "I will hear what God the Lord will speak, For He will speak peace to His people and to His saints."

One of the devil's tactics against God's people knowing who they are is distraction and busyness. Do not ask God to fit into a small window of your schedule. Do not give Him the crumbs of your time. Learn to prioritize time with your heavenly Father so you can intentionally listen to His quiet, still small voice reminding you daily of who and whose you are.

Then, in addition, take time to meditate (consider, ponder, think deeply upon) what His Word says about you and your identity in Christ. I provided a list of many of these in this book on pages 3 & 4 of chapter 1.

God knew this war would be raging over our identity, our value, and our worth so He sent His Word to heal us (Psalm 107:20). Consider this though: You can have a medicine in your hand and believe it will heal you, but if you do not take it, it will do you no good. Looking at it on the shelf will not help. Just saying you will take it won't help either. <u>Medicine must be received and applied for healing.</u> Take God's Word – written and living – and make time to feed on it.

You will find once you hear God whisper, "I love you," worry fades. Once you see in the Bible that God's purpose required your existence and that you are fearfully and wonderfully made, anxiety or depression begin to slowly subside and purpose begins to rise! Situations and circumstances of life can be difficult, but because we take time to bathe ourselves in our Father's written and spoken Word, we can stand firm upon the Rock of our salvation while the storms rage.

John 8:31-32 "31 Then Jesus said to those who believed on Him, 'If you abide (live, remain, stay) in My word, you are My disciples indeed, 32 And you shall know the truth and the truth shall make you free.'"

In John 8:36 Jesus adds, "If, therefore, the Son makes you free, you are free indeed."

In John 10:27 Jesus says, "My sheep know My voice, I know them, and they follow Me."

Jesus wants you intimately acquainted with His voice AND His Word. Do not let random Bible reading take the place of hearing the voice of the Shepherd. Let the Bible confirm, add to, and bring balance to what you hear personally from the Lord. After all, Jesus is not going to tell you something that disputes or refutes the Scriptures.

In Matthew 4 Jesus said "Man does not live by bread alone, but by every word that <u>proceeds</u> from the mouth of God." 'Proceeds' here is in the ongoing, present tense. It does not say we live "by every word that proceeded…" So do not just live by what your heavenly Father said to you last week or last year, but by what He speaks to you each day. Listening to God speak only so often will not yield the fruit you want to see.

A little advice – as you listen in prayer, listen softly from within, Christ is present in you and more than likely is not going to speak to you audibly from some Galaxy far, far away.

Also, when the Lord says good things to you, don't argue with Him about how bad you are. Titus 1:2 says God cannot lie. Humble yourself and receive what He says. Feed on it. It's life and health to you.

Tool #2: No more earning, only resting.

The Lord told me once, "Steve, when Christians stop living like they're earning something, and start living like they've received something, they can change the world." We have been taught to earn our love, our wages, our blessings, and even our grades from God. The obvious impossibility of carrying out such a moral program should make it plain that no one can sustain a relationship with God that way. The person who lives in right relationship with God does it by embracing what God has done for him rather than what he's done for God. Doing things FOR God to earn points or favors is the opposite of entering into what God has done FOR you. The person who walks closely with God simply believes he has been set right BY GOD – not by his own moral efforts.

Philippians 2:12-13 says, "12 So then, my beloved, just as you have always obeyed, not as in my presence only, but now much more

**in my absence, work OUT your salvation
with fear and trembling; 13 <u>for it is God who
is at work in you,</u> both to will and to work
for His good pleasure....**

Paul doesn't say work FOR your salvation, but
merely work OUT your salvation! Then he adds
for it is God who is at work IN you, so partner
with Him!

<u>Tool #3: Be a friend to yourself and choose to
hang around folks who see you as God does.</u>

**1 Corinthians 15:33 says, "Do not be misled,
bad company corrupts good character."**

Authentic human relationship is a must. We are
truly made for it as we see in Genesis 2:18. But
be wise and steer away from people who accept
or reject you solely according to your behavior
and cannot see your true identity in Christ.
Those who label and perceive you as less than
God's view of you may not be the best of
friends, or dare I say it – church members. Yes
I do recommend you try and locate a church
family that sees, knows, and teaches new
creation identity.

Who we spend time with is crucial because who
we hang out with is so often who we become

like. If you are considering marriage, marry someone who agrees with God about your identity and value. When you do something incongruent with your true identity, they will partner with you in restoring you – not just reject and discard you.

Being in covenant together means you and your spouse are committed for the long haul. How else can we help each other overcome our shortcomings and deficiencies and point each other toward wholeness instead of shame? Each of you need to mature to the point of saying, "I do not know you by what you just did wrong, I know you by Who lives within you by His Spirit."

As for friends and which ones can be healthy; examine whether you are doing the influencing or the one being influenced. Are you a thermometer, which just reflects the climate of the room you're in, or are you a thermostat – the one setting the climate in the room.

Tool #4: Guard your heart against offense.

Hebrews 12:15 says, "Looking carefully lest anyone fall short of the grace of God; lest any root of bitterness springing up cause trouble, for by this many become defiled..."

Nothing renders believers more unfruitful or honestly, more unhealthy, than offense and hidden resentments. Goodwill always triumphs ill-will in my view because the first half of the word "ill-will" is ill! It definitely keynotes that if a human stays in a resentment too long, it can make them sick. One doctor said he knew of no single thing that wreaked more havoc on the human body than offense and hidden resentments.

I find it fascinating that neither the true you of your spirit man nor your physical body can thrive in bitterness. I believe this again gives credence to the Scripture that we as humans are made by God and FOR God. What looks good and right on Him is going to be good and right for us! When I look at Jesus who is the expressed image of God's nature (Hebrews 1:3), I don't see offense, bitterness, or resentments; I see love, forgiveness, and compassion. We simply cannot live at odds with the nature of God without getting hurt. Not because God will hurt us, but because hurt seems built into living life against our design. The bottom line is: You and I are made for the identity and new nature we have in Christ.

Just because we do not thrive in offense or grudges, doesn't change the fact the flesh part of us can be easily offended. Try not to take things your spouse or anyone else does wrong personally, causing a reaction in the flesh. Remember you and your spouse have a common enemy who hates your marriage covenant and hates each of you. Set your mind to proactively walk in the spirit towards your spouse so you are prepared ahead of time for any of their missteps. This way, when your spouse or even your child does a big piece of stupid, you can partner with God and remind them of who they are in Christ.

Communicate to your son or daughter their value is <u>not</u> determined by their performance. Yes, their recent wrong behavior was perhaps a 3 out of 10 and should be met with some form of discipline, but they are still a 10 out of 10 in value, identity, and worth as a child of God. And because we know and see they are a 10, we love them too much to let them live as a 3.

Tool #5: Remember Christ is IN you!

Galatians 2:20 says, "It is no longer I that live, but Christ lives in me."

Once you invite Christ into your life, live like He's actually there. <u>Why would God place Christ inside of us only to be a spectator?</u> Christ is in you to live through you. Do not strive to be good. Participate with God's goodness already in you in Christ. Do not strive to be holy. Participate with God's holiness already present within you in Christ. Do not strive to love. Participate with God's love already present in you in Christ. Christ and His character traits are present in us; therefore, we don't have to work for God's goodness, holiness, and love, we can work with them!!

Pastor Steve Eden

Chapter 8
Sanctification By Identification

Sanctification is the process whereby a Christian becomes more and more like Christ in their thoughts, character, emotions, and actions. Historically, to sanctify also means, "to set apart; to make holy or sacred."

1 Thessalonians 4:3 says, "This is God's will, your sanctification."

There should be no debating that sanctification is biblical and very much part of God's will for our lives. Don't let people tell you God doesn't care whether we are growing and maturing into the image of Christ. The question however, centers on how to go about it.

We often try to change our wrong behaviors via self effort or "won't power" instead of simply participating with and agreeing with our new creation identity. I call the fruit of this agreement, "sanctification by identification." Our behavior gets transformed through our simple agreement with how holy and righteous God has made us.

Unfortunately, we've been taught that the goal

of the Christian life is "sin management" instead of discovering the truth of who and whose we are through intimacy with God. Yet, even the best way to manage sin is to identify and agree with the identity God gave to us! If we want to grow in sanctification, we should not be looking at ourselves and our sin all the time but at Christ and who He is in us. Try these 3 easy steps: 1- Wake up. 2- Remember who you are. 3- Go be a new creation in Christ.

1 Corinthians 1:30 says, "But of Him you are in Christ Jesus, who <u>became for us</u> wisdom from God—and righteousness and <u>sanctification</u> and redemption."

Christ within is literally our sanctification. He leads us, guides us, and directs us into the truth of who we are, always there to remind us should we veer off course. Not to mention, the more He lives through us, the more holiness is seen and revealed through us. I often say, "Christ is a better Christian than we are, so we should LET His Spirit live, love, and serve through us."

It's simply the power of "Let"! "Let" the word of Christ dwell in you richly (Colossians 3:16). "Let" God arise and His enemies be scattered (Psalm 68:1). "Let" this same mind be in you which was also in Christ Jesus (Philippians 2:5). <u>Christianity should be much more centered on the indwelling of Christ than the imitation of Christ.</u>

2 Thessalonians 2:13 says, "But we are bound to give thanks to God always for you, brethren beloved by the Lord, because God from the beginning chose you for salvation through <u>sanctification by the Spirit and belief in the truth.</u>"

It is clear that our process of becoming more and more like Christ in conduct and character comes "<u>by the Spirit and belief in the truth.</u>" Think about that—in order to live more holy, we simply partner with the Spirit and BELIEVE in the truth! That is a far cry from using our own abilities to "stop sinning" in order to make ourselves holy.

1 Corinthians 15:34 says, "Awaken unto Righteousness and sin not."

Notice which one comes first! I do not stop sinning so I can now believe I am righteous; I discover how righteous I am and as a result I sin not. It is sanctification by identification! God makes you holy through Christ as a gift, so that through your simple faith in what He's done, you live a holy life. Religion and the world say what you do determines who you are, but God says let who you are determine what you do.

How crucial is it for you see to yourself as pure and clean in Christ? If you have two rooms in your house and one is filthy with trash all over the floor and one is clean and spotless, which room do you think you would be more at ease putting trash in? That's right – the filthy one. Not many people are willing to throw trash in a clean and spotless room but if the room is already dirty it's like, "What's a little more trash?" Friend, dare to believe how pure and clean you are in Christ and notice immediately how empowered you are to say no to those "unclean" temptations we all face!

So who do you think is behind convincing you that you are a lowly nobody? Satan is. As long as you think you are a worthless worm, you will act out that reality. On the other hand, if you agree with how holy God says you are, you will act out His Reality. Once again, our behavior is simply a byproduct of what we believe about ourselves. Our deed reveals our creed. Righteousness in root, righteousness in fruit.

If it is true "as a man thinks in his heart so is he..." then no wonder God had to convince us we were righteous before He could ever get us to live that way. How does He convince us? By bypassing our performance and giving us righteousness and holiness as a gift through Christ-- a gift that is received not earned. Then, from our place of security in Christ, we simply begin growing in our knowing of who He says we are as His beloved children and His precious new creations!!

Galatians 5:16 says if you align your mind with who you are by the Spirit, you won't fulfill the lust of the flesh. You will live and act holy because you believe and know and see yourself as holy.

In John 17:17 Jesus said, "Sanctify them in truth, thy Word is Truth."

Saints of God will live much holier lives by hearing more and more truth about who they are in Christ than they ever will hearing they are just unholy, undeserving sinners saved by grace. It's amazing how when holiness is taught as the byproduct of their relationship with God rather than the basis of their relationship how much empowerment they receive.

To 'repent' means to literally change your mind and your perspective, to change how you think.

Accordingly, Romans 12:2 says, "Do not be conformed to this world but be transformed by the <u>renewing of your mind,</u> that you may prove how good, acceptable, and perfect God's will is."

Paul wrote that to Christians! So it's very possible for followers of Christ to look and act like the world. How does that happen? We don't renew our minds to agree with who God says we are.

2 Corinthians 5:14 says, "The love of Christ constrains us."

Sanctification and self-control is a fruit of God's Spirit. His unconditional love and His unfailing presence give you self-control. Yielding to God transforms the way we respond to temptation, ourselves, and others. God's Spirit restrains us and re-trains us. <u>When walking in love, we not only no longer steal from others, God's Spirit causes us to want to give to and even bless others</u>. God's Spirit restrains us from adultery for example by giving us God's perspective about the sacredness of marriage; as well as how the sin of adultery could destroy other people, families, and children.

Some aids in your sanctification:

1- <u>Stop waiting to get good enough for God to use you</u>. Honestly, we can't wait that long! He wants to use you now – yes, just as you are. I realize you have flaws and weaknesses, but you have Jesus power working in you and through you. He will address your flaws as you keep your eyes on Him. In the meantime, let's make the world a better place!

2- <u>Stop trying to qualify yourself</u>. God already qualified you by putting His Spirit within you as a new creation. Colossians 2:10 says you are complete (adequate, qualified) in Him. Christ within is all the qualification you need to begin helping others.

3- <u>Understand God's win-win ability</u>. God has a great power to turn our failures into successes. The way God sees it - humans are like grapes. When we get squeezed by life's frustrations and trials, whatever is inside us is going to come out. So if ugliness comes out, He will use that to reveal to us areas He still needs to touch, heal, and grow. That is a win. If we are squeezed by life and beauty comes out, He will use it to reveal to us our growth and development. That is a win as well.

4- <u>Learn to enjoy what God's grace has given you</u>. You came from the womb a sinner in need of a Savior. Now you have received the Savior, so stop limiting Him to what He saved you <u>from</u>. Let Him bring you into the inheritance He saved you <u>for</u>: Intimacy with Christ, peace, joy, freedom, love, righteousness, and liberty. Dance with those things!

5- <u>Understand basic math and the power of two against one</u>. Each day there is God's spirit, your mind, and the flesh all at work in you and your decisions. If you align your mind with the flesh that makes two on one against the spirit and you will manifest deeds of the flesh. If you align your mind with God's spirit, that makes two on one against the flesh and you will manifest the fruit of the spirit.

Romans 8:5-6 says, "For those who live according to the flesh <u>set their minds</u> on the things of the flesh, but those *who live* according to the Spirit, <u>set their minds</u> on the things of the Spirit. 6 For to be carnally minded *is* death, but to be spiritually minded *is* life and peace."

The answer is right there in Romans 8:5-6. How do some people actually live according to and by the Spirit? They set their MINDS on the things of the Spirit. Well why do people get locked into living by the flesh? They set their MINDS on the things of the flesh.

Pastor Steve Eden

Chapter 9
Answering THE Question:

So Why Should I Live Holy?

As the people of God, we serve a "Holy" God, we read what is called a "Holy" Bible, we get filled with what is called the "Holy" Spirit, and we get labeled by God Himself a "Holy" nation; so the idea of living a "holy" life is nothing to scoff at.

In this chapter, I thought I would answer the question that I am occasionally asked -- "If I am already made righteous in my spirit, and God loves me no matter what, why does it even matter if I live a holy or upright life?"

1) Because that is who we are!

I've covered this one at length in this book, but how 'bout one more scripture for good measure??

Colossians 3:12 says, "Therefore, <u>AS *the* elect of God, holy and beloved</u>, put on tender mercies, kindness, humility, meekness, longsuffering…"

Notice Paul says, "AS the elect of God, holy and beloved, put on tender mercies," he does not say, "SO you can be the elect of God, holy and beloved, put on tender mercies." He is simply saying because you are holy, because that's your true identity, do what is right.

2) Because the Bible instructs us to live holy lives.

1 Peter 1:13-16 says, "13 Therefore gird up the loins of your mind, be sober, and rest *your* hope fully upon the grace that is to be brought to you at the revelation of Jesus Christ; 14 as obedient children, not conforming yourselves to the former lusts, *as* in your ignorance; 15 but as He who called you *is* holy, you also be holy in all *your* conduct, 16 because it is written, "Be holy, for I am holy."

I see this instruction to be holy as I am holy not as rigid and burdensome but as a good Father saying to his child, "I simply want you to be like me." Jesus rebuked the Pharisees for laying up heavy loads on people but not lifting a finger to help them. Your Heavenly Father is not like that. He understands when He says, "Be Holy for I am holy" that He will need to supply the Holiness. Therefore holiness is not something I am trying to live up to, it's something I get to live out of.

Also again notice 1 Peter 1:14 says "AS God's obedient children...be holy," not "SO you can be God's obedient children!" Even though what you do outwardly does not change who you are inwardly; your spirit man says, "Now in Christ I'm empowered to act outwardly in accordance with what Jesus did inwardly!"

These next two Scriptures support God's call on us to manifest His holiness:

1 Thessalonians 4:7 says, "For God has not called us unto uncleanness, but unto holiness."

2 Timothy 1:9 says, "God has saved us, and called us with a holy calling, not according to our works, but according to his own purpose and grace, which was given us in Christ Jesus before the world began."

It is clear we are not called unto holiness by what we do, but by what God has done. Mankind, from the beginning, was called to holiness through intimacy with God. As I have said before, it sure fits us and our spirit, soul, and body better than unholiness does.

3) Because we love God.

In John 14:15 Jesus says, "If you love Me, keep My commands."

Notice Jesus didn't say, "If you want to be holy, keep my commands." Or "If you don't want Me to give you sickness, keep My commands." He's simply saying "If you want to show Me love, this is how you love Me – keep My commands."

If Jesus were here in the flesh, we would all approach Him and very humbly express our love and gratitude to Him in all kinds of ways. Knowing He would not be here in the flesh, He left us a way we can demonstrate our love and gratitude – keep His commands to love.

One command is John 13:34 where Jesus said, "A new command I give you, that you love one another just like I love you." So when we walk in love for our fellow believers, we show love for Christ. Which makes a lot of sense because in Matthew 25:40 Jesus said, "That which you do to the least of these My brethren, you do unto Me." How is that possible? Christ lives inside each and every believer, so when we love each other, we are indeed loving Him.

1 John 5:3 says, "This is the love of God that we keep His commands and His commands are not burdensome."

Again we see that keeping the Lord's commands is a way we show love to God. It's not how we can convince God we are holy, it is how we can express love to Him. It's not how we convince God not to send us to hell, it's how we give the love He first gave to us back to Him.

4) Because we love people.

I will never forget being in a Sunday morning church service and the Lord telling me He was opposed to sin because of how it hurts and harms people! Talk about an eye opener! I always thought God opposed sin because… Are you ready… **It was wrong!!** I never once thought it had to do with how sin destroys the homes, families, individuals, and marriages that God so dearly loves.

Romans 13:8-10 says, "8 Owe no one anything except to love one another, for he who loves another has fulfilled the law.

9 For the commandments, "You shall not commit adultery," "You shall not murder," "You shall not steal," "You shall not bear false witness," "You shall not covet," and if *there is* any other commandment, are *all* summed up in this saying, namely, "You shall love your neighbor as yourself."
10 Love does no harm to a neighbor; therefore love *is* the fulfillment of the law."

As you can see, the underlying principle/goal of the Old Testament law given to Israel was loving others. We know that sinning against people is not loving them: taking someone's wife, taking their money, or slandering them is not love. It is not faith or trust in God's provision either. Galatians 5:6 says, "Faith works through love." They go hand in hand.

God commanded the people of Israel not to commit adultery because it was not love to take their neighbor's spouse or be disloyal to their own; yet someone having an affair might say, "But God, I love her." No he only thinks he loves her; and certainly he does not love her husband, his own wife, her kids, his kids, or the testimony of Jesus. Based on Scripture, you cannot convince me that any act of adultery originates in or involves "love".

5) Because we don't want to cause others to stumble.

1 Corinthians 8:13 says, "Therefore, if food makes my brother stumble, I won't eat meat again."

Notice Paul didn't say, "I'm not going to eat meat so I can be holy," he simply said he does not want to do things that could hurt other believers. **Simply put, God values love over liberty.** Yes, you're free to do as you like, after all you are forever righteous and forgiven in Christ in your spirit, but never use your freedom to hurt others. *Galatians 5:13 says, "My brothers and sisters, you were called to be free. But do not use your freedom to indulge the flesh; rather, serve one another in love."*

Ladies, dressing modestly won't make you more holy but it can demonstrate you love your brother in Christ who may struggle with lustful thoughts. Guys, I understand you can have a beer here or there and be ok, but if the guy you're having a beer with is an alcoholic, you may be tempting him. Having right doctrine will not always equate in righteous behavior but walking in the love of Christ towards others will.

6) Because sin has wages on it.

Romans 6:23 says, "For the wages of sin is death, but the gift of God is eternal life through Jesus Christ our Lord."

Let me be very clear: Jesus took all the punishment for our sin; He totally and completely satisfied God's wrath against it, but He did not nullify the earthly consequences of sin! Take it from me and countless other human beings who've been on this planet long enough to mess up, sin will try to destroy and/or take everything you love in this natural world. Sin can bring death in the 'here & now' just as it can in the 'hereafter'.

Here's what you need to know about why our behavior matters and why it is important we agree with who God says we are. Sin is unhealthy, unnatural, and unsatisfying.

1 Peter 2:11 says, "Beloved, I beg you as sojourners and pilgrims, abstain from fleshly lusts <u>that war against the soul.</u>"

Take the top 3 strongholds here in Eastern Oklahoma County: Prescription drug addiction, Meth addiction, and Domestic Violence – are any of those healthy, natural, or satisfying to the human soul? Of course not. Christians and atheists would both agree on that. Will any of those behaviors make a born again Christian unholy? No, but could those things kill them? Destroy their family? Absolutely. Could they war against their soul, their mind, their emotions? Yes indeed.

1 Corinthians 10:23 says, "All things are lawful, but not all things are profitable. All things are lawful, but not all things edify."

Paul is saying here we are indeed free from the law of performance based acceptance and earned righteousness, but we should be very careful what activities we choose. There is no doubt sin is not profitable for human beings physically, emotionally, financially, or mentally.

On the other hand, Christ and His loving and pure-hearted ways are!! <u>When is the last time you heard someone say, "Man I wish I hadn't spent all weekend with Jesus -- loving Him, caring about others, reading His Word – now I feel so hungover, worthless, and used up</u>." Sin will always be under the law of diminishing returns, Christ and His ways will not.

7) To inspire others.

Matthew 5:16 says, "Let your light so shine before men, that they may see your good works and glorify your Father in Heaven."

Jesus says His light shining through you can cause people to glorify God! Our goodness and kindness can help reveal God and His Presence in this world. Imagine living upright not so God will love us but to simply reflect Christ to others. How wonderful when someone says, "I want WHO that guy has!"

As living epistles, we need to always be mindful that our actions are an opportunity for Christ to be seen in and through us. Perhaps you can make this part of your daily prayer, "Lord, when people see me, may they see you."

Chapter 10
The End of the Journey or Just the Beginning?

I pray this book has been a most rewarding journey of discovery for you! I pray your walk with Christ has been so greatly enhanced that today marks not an end but a brand new beginning! A beginning where you live daily with the truth, the Spirit, and the recognition Christ is internally and eternally present with you— leading you, guiding you, loving you, and empowering you to His great ends!

There are a couple of bottom lines to this book. The first bottom line is belief. As long as you live life actively believing that God loves you without condition, that you are holy and righteous through Christ, and that all your sins have been forgiven, wouldn't that affect your behavior in a positive and Godly way? Of course it would. <u>Then we don't really have a behavior problem in the body of Christ, as much as we have a belief problem.</u>

Yet for at least the last 200 years, guess what the church has majored in? You guessed it -- "behavior modification." I believe we will be better served if our focus is simply belief in the truth. That is what I have invited you to do: Dare to believe the truth of what God says about you no matter how good it is!

Pride in its purest form is simply exalting your view of you over God's view of you. Purpose each day then to humbly exalt the truth of God's Word above all other realities and perspectives. Don't let the good news of a righteous identity Jesus intended for all His followers be in vain! We honor Him far more by believing we are clean and righteous than we do by telling Him we are no good nobody's.

The second bottom line of this book is proper value assignment. Do you assign more value to what God says about you, or what others say? Do you assign more value to what God says about you or to how you feel? By now you should recognize God's love for you is greater than your mistakes. You should be able to see how Christ's blood is greater than your missteps. All in all, your future in God is greater than your past – whether your past was ten years ago, ten days ago, or even ten minutes ago!

It is hard for the world to conquer a heart that's already been conquered. It is hard for circumstances to overtake a heart that's already overtaken. It is hard for lies to get into a heart that's already filled up with truth! The truth of God's Word renews our minds, transforms our hearts, and aligns us with our true identity and value.

<u>You simply must see that you are not who you used to be.</u> You can admonish saints of God not to fornicate. You can instruct a child of God not to lie, but you can't tell sinners not to do those things because they will do them -- that's who they are by nature. You invite a sinner to get born again, to receive the nature of Christ within, not to stop sinning. Once they are born again though, will they be tempted? Yes of course. But now you can encourage them, "Brother, don't go back to your old ways, because that is no longer WHO YOU ARE!"

Ephesians 4:22-24 says, "22 You put off, concerning your former conduct, the old man which grows corrupt according to the deceitful lusts, 23 and be renewed in the spirit of your mind, 24 and <u>put on the new man which was created according to God, in true righteousness and holiness.</u>"

You are not the same person you were before you got saved. Yet do you know how many

93

people go to church their whole life and never hear they have a "new man" remade in God's righteousness? They struggle mightily because it's hard to put on your new man if you were never told you had one.

Your journey as a Christian is a growth process. Salvation is just the beginning not the end. We hear a few truths, get saved, see some light, start believing and agreeing; but it's imperative we continue growing in our knowing of our new creation identity through the whole process.

Satan's biggest crime he has ever perpetrated against the saints of God is identity theft; deceiving and blinding them from ever fully seeing who they really are in Christ. His first goal is to keep us from being saved, but then once we are, his goal is to keep us from ever discovering who God the Father made us inwardly at our new birth.

With that, I leave you with a list of "firewalls" that will empower you, keep you secure, and keep your mind renewed along your journey of intimacy with Christ.

Firewalls of Truth that keep you from being moved off the true you:

1) God cannot lie (Titus 1:2)
2) The truest thing about you is what God says about you (3 John 1:4)
3) If your view of you does not match God's view of you, then you are wrong
4) Just because you think, feel, or believe something about yourself does not make it true (2 Corinthians 5:7)
5) Just because you choose not to believe something good that God says about you does not make it untrue
6) Agreeing with who God says you are is an act of humility, not pride (1 Peter 5:5)
7) If knowing the truth sets you free, then believing a lie will set you into bondage (John 8:32)
8) Know and see yourself as God already does, by the Spirit, not by your flesh (2 Corinthians 5:16; 21)
9) Once you're born again, you do not get to determine who/what you are, you only get to discover who/what you are by the Holy Spirit (1 Corinthians 2:12-14)
10) What you do does not make you who you are; what God has done IN you makes you who you are (2 Corinthians 5:17)
11) Your performance doesn't determine what is true about you, it only determines whether you experience the life/peace of what is true about you

Pastor Steve Eden

ABOUT THE AUTHOR

At the age of 20, Steve Eden had a personal encounter with Jesus Christ while attending Northeastern (OK) State University. Feeling burned out and like a complete failure as a young Christian, it was in that encounter Jesus told him, "Steve, I love you because of who I am not because of what you do. So I want you to live the rest of your life from My love and not for it."

From that time on, with the Holy Spirit's guidance, Steve has been on a journey to bring himself and others out of performance based Christianity and into a vibrant, present tense, intimate relationship with his Lord, Savior, Best Friend, and Sanctifier Jesus Christ.